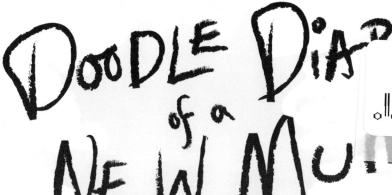

DOODLE DIARY
of a
NEW MUM

AN ILLUSTRATED JOURNEY THROUGH ONE MUMMY'S FIRST YEAR

by Lucy Scott

RUNNING PRESS
PHILADELPHIA · LONDON

For my darling Lois, so longed for and precious; her wonderful dad Tom, my hero; and for my own consistently brilliant mum and dad.

Thanks also to Isabel Atherton, Jordana Tusman, and Sarah Pierson for taking a chance on me and working so hard on my behalf.

Books published by Running Press are available at special discounts for bulk purchases in the United States by corporations, institutions, and other organisations. For more information, please contact the Special Markets Department at the Perseus Books Group, 2300 Chestnut Street, Suite 200, Philadelphia, PA 19103, or call (800) 810-4145, ext. 5000, or e-mail special.markets@perseusbooks.com.

ISBN 978-0-7624-5685-7

9   8   7   6   5   4   3   2
Digit on the right indicates the number of this printing

Cover and interior design by Sarah Pierson
Edited by Jordana Tusman
Typography: Aunt Mildred, Avenir, and Flyerfonts

Running Press Book Publishers
2300 Chestnut Street
Philadelphia, PA 19103-4371

Visit us on the web!
www.runningpress.com

INTRODUCTION

IN JULY 2012, I gave birth to a lovely little girl, who we called Lois.

For me, the learning curve of parenthood was a ludicrously steep one, made all the more difficult to climb with stitches in, ahem, private places, yo-yoing hormones, and suffering from the kind of sleep deprivation normally reserved for chronic insomniacs.

For those of you who are bringing up your baby alone or effectively alone, or for those of you that have more than one child, I stand erect in my best outfit and salute you—or bow as low as my belly allows, whichever you'd prefer. Even with a lovely, very involved bloke by my side, my precious, wonderful baby can have me whimpering on my knees.

I did know it would be a full-time, forever job, but I didn't anticipate that for a year hot food would become a luxury, going to the loo a mission, and maintaining socially acceptable personal hygiene levels a challenge. It's tough; I miss my partner even though I pass him regularly in the hall.

Compelled to preserve my memories forever, I started drawing. And so emerged my *Doodle Diary of a New Mum*.

Now my baby is a few months away from turning two and I only vaguely remember a world before sticky carpets, a world where I wore make-up every day, blow-dried my hair, had nice nails, and a handbag that wasn't filled with mashed banana and raisins.

But it is impossible to grumble when somehow I have in part created the most wonderful little person that I ever could have imagined, a feisty wee girl full of character, humor, and kindness. Who'd swap that for nice nails?!

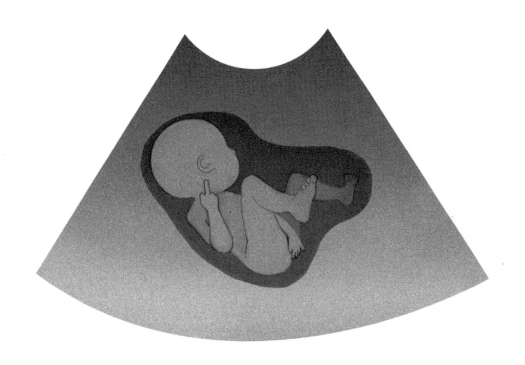

Gender Scan

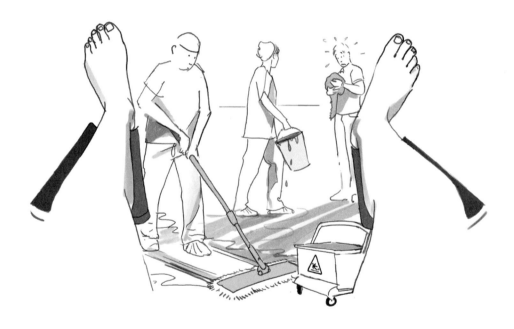

The Birth

My Beautiful Baby

Recommendation: Do not wrap a naked baby in a family heirloom.

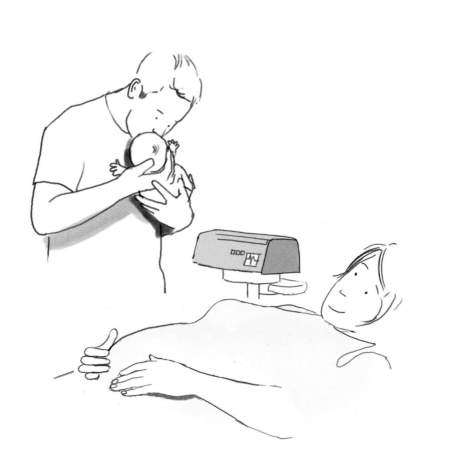

We love you very much, but your belly button stinks!

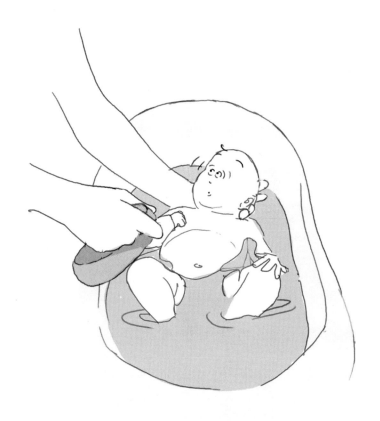

If you let me go, I will never forget.

Actual Torture

Small Victories!

First Lunch Out

First trip to the health visitor . . . la la la.

Aaaggghhhhhhh!

Friday nights are not quite the same.

Sleep training: Introduce a lovey.

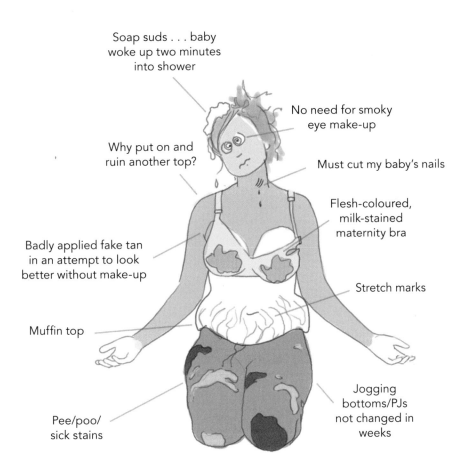

Soap suds . . . baby woke up two minutes into shower

No need for smoky eye make-up

Why put on and ruin another top?

Must cut my baby's nails

Badly applied fake tan in an attempt to look better without make-up

Flesh-coloured, milk-stained maternity bra

Stretch marks

Muffin top

Pee/poo/sick stains

Jogging bottoms/PJs not changed in weeks

Having a baby doesn't change you.

New Shoes

Being trapped under a sleeping baby in a dark room
only increases the potential to spend.

A Truly Extraordinary Poo

Spontaneous trip out: Approximately 45 minutes to get out the door.

Behold the shrine to wet wipes.

Sleep training: As baby drifts off, gently remove breast.

Bullseye

Note: Do not apply fake tan and then breast-feed.

Time for a nap.

Is there such a thing as mummy nappies?

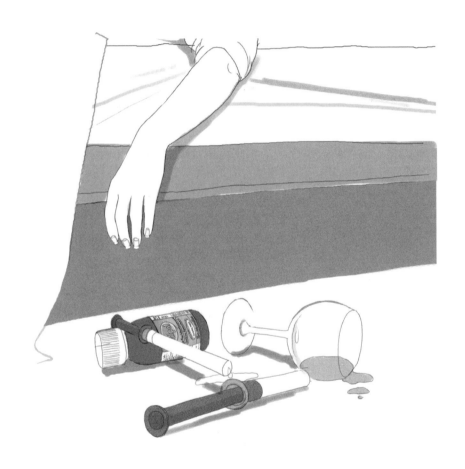

Heavy Night

Asking a little too much of concealer!

What?! HOW?!

After an unusually relaxing bath. . . .

Ball Poolitis

That'll do it.

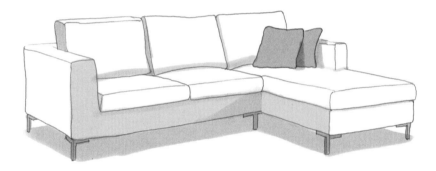

Come in and have a seat on my lovely couch.

Forensic view of couch: snot, pee, poo, and sick.

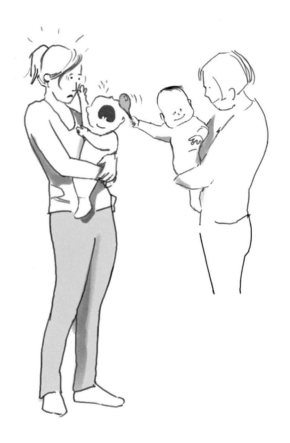

Playgroup Maraca Assault

Well, that's you packed. I'll just take a change of pants.

Please, my darling, I'll give you the car,
the house, everything, just please stop crying.

If a look could say,
Turn that on and I'll kill you.

First Immunisations

The rabbit started it.

Muslins? What could I possibly need these for?

Four months later . . .

Noooooooo! I forgot to bring the muslin!

The Great Sophie the Giraffe Germ Lottery

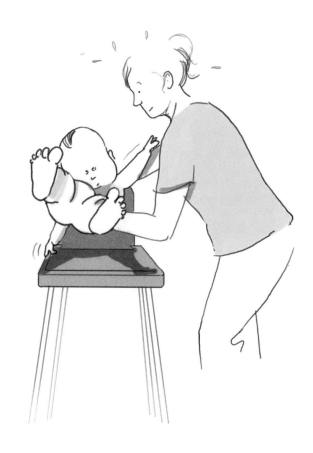

High Chair Gymnastics

How can your stomach muscles do that?!

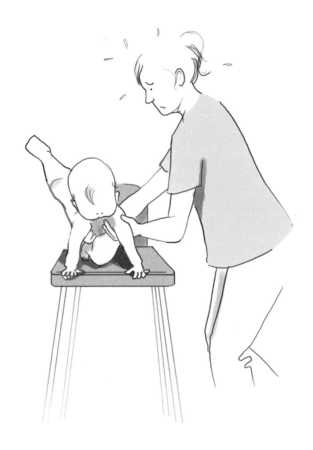

Oh good grief!

Put one end in baby's nose and then do WHAT?!?!

NO!

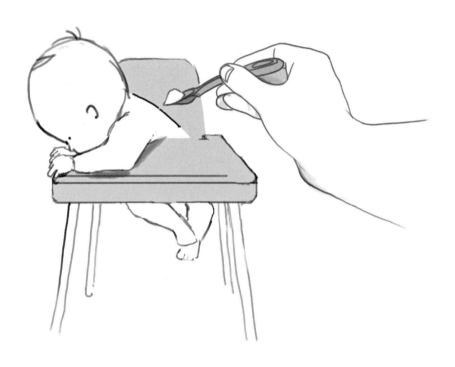

I said NO!

Ah, banana, you should have said.

Trying to make a quiet exit.

Feeling Sexy

Love, Granny x

Hold . . .

As I thought . . . no.

Don't wrestle a baby, you'll lose.

The Two-Finger-Up-the-Nose Takedown

How early is too early?

New Friends

The Joy of Long Car Journeys

Packaging: It really is true.

Enough of this silliness, Mummy . . . just give me YOUR phone.

Stair gate: how to push a mummy over the edge.

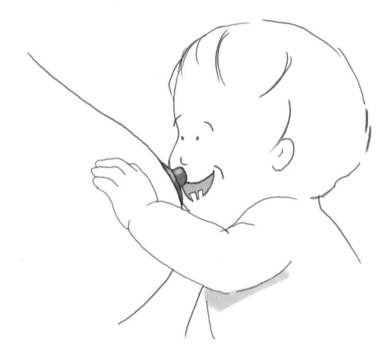

All I can see is TEETH!

Naked Time = Poo Roulette

Oh, you've bought her a drum . . . excellent . . .

We'd love to come but our baby is very unwell. . . .

How to Clear a Pub

How to Depress a Restaurant

My living room at 7.00 a.m.

7.12 a.m. . . . someone's up!

Health and Safety

Soooo Sleepy

Texting in Order for Lunch

Solids introduced: Oh my dear god!

Every SINGLE Trip Out

OK, so where are your _____?
(insert as applicable)

Hmmm, poppers.

Superbaby!

What?

Public toilets, skinny jeans, and a baby are a sweaty mix.

Erm . . . the *on* button, I know this.

Weighing the pros and cons of daddy making dinner.

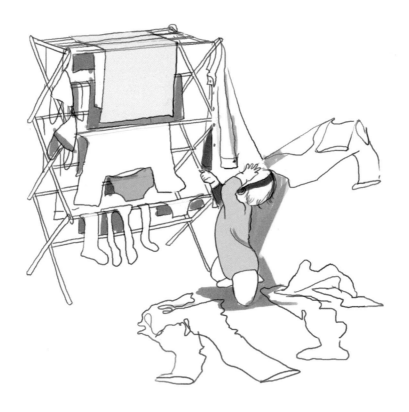

Busy, Busy

Thank you, so helpful.

Date Night

Grandad's Remote Control

Granny's Glasses

Obligatory Bathtime Hairstyle

Confidence Boost

One spoonful, two, three, seven, five. . . .

No Shame

Second trip to the health visitor . . . la la la.

Aaaggghhhhhh!

Yes, I know it's too small for you, but it was very expensive!

NOTHING is more interesting than a wee box of raisins.

A technique guaranteed NEVER to work.

Two minutes till party time.

A Night Out with Old Friends

Whoa there!!

And the prize for Mum of the Year goes to. . . .

There will be no money shot today.

And the rest of the day is your own. . . .

Baby's Portrait of a Mummy

You Today

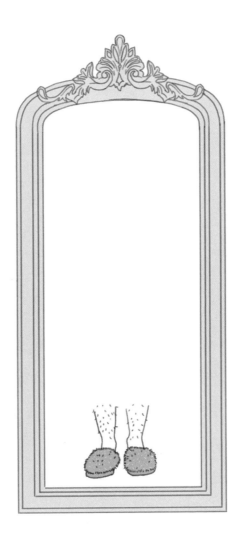

If you're looking and feeling great, spend the time you would
have spent doodling this giving yourself a round of applause.

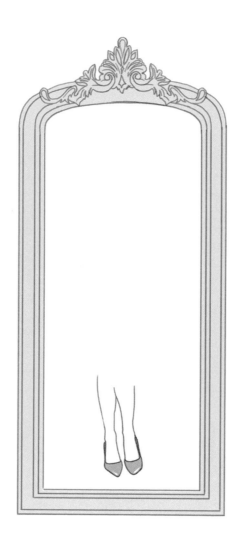

You in One Year

We've been very lucky with our little Octavia. She's slept through the night since six weeks and walked at nine months. Yesterday she counted to ten in Mandarin. We have no idea where she picked that up!

Your reply. . . .

Create Supermum

Some Ideas:

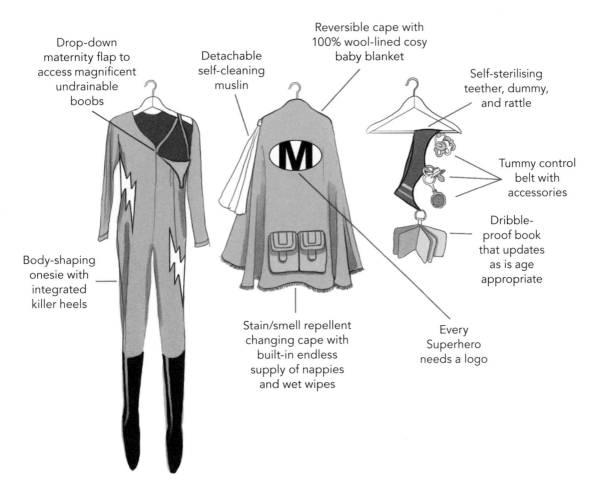

Drop-down maternity flap to access magnificent undrainable boobs

Detachable self-cleaning muslin

Reversible cape with 100% wool-lined cosy baby blanket

Self-sterilising teether, dummy, and rattle

Tummy control belt with accessories

Dribble-proof book that updates as is age appropriate

Body-shaping onesie with integrated killer heels

Stain/smell repellent changing cape with built-in endless supply of nappies and wet wipes

Every Superhero needs a logo

M

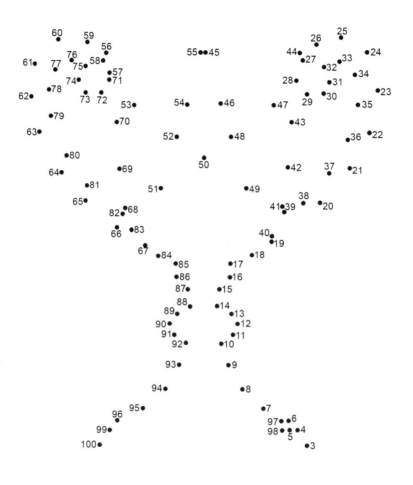

You deserve it!